MW01593269

Dreamstreet

All profits derived from the sale of this book
will be donated to:

Providence House
Domestic Violence Services
Ocean County, New Jersey

Dreamstreet

The poetry of
Thom Cherney
&
Nicole Dietrich

Cover and artwork by
Sammantha Dietrich
&
Donald Botticelli

Thom The Janitor

Library of Congress Control Number: 2009907647
ISBN: Hardcover   978-1-4415-5934-0
                 Softcover   978-1-4415-5933-3

This book was printed in the United States of America.

To order additional copies of this book, contact:
Xlibris Corporation
1-888-795-4274
www.Xlibris.com
Orders@Xlibris.com
66593

Contents

The Poems of Thom Cherney

1.	All fall down	11
2.	Angels walk the hall	12
3.	As summer grows nigh	13
4.	As we travel	14
5.	At the back door	15
6.	Bring in the clown	16
7.	For roseanne	17
8.	My Minds Eye	19
9.	My brother never cried	20
10.	My poems	21
11.	My words	22
12.	Parallel realities	23
13.	Perchance	25
14.	Please don't fight	26
15.	Rolling thunder	28
16.	Second - Hand pencils	29
17.	The runner	30
18.	The man	32
19.	The fall of man	33
20.	Mankind today	35
21.	The path of peace	37
22.	The School Hallway	38
23.	Hypocrites	39
24.	The worn "T" shirt	40
25.	Trail of tears	41
26.	What i have seen	42
27.	Why?	43
28.	"Whys and Therefores"	46
29.	Reality	47
30.	I awoke	48

31. I'll walk to the river 49
32. The Doorkeeper 51
33. The Doorkeeper 52
34. Mortality 54
35. To bow at the altar of conformity 55

The Poems of Nicole Dietrich
36. Untitled 56
37. Untitled 57
38. Untitled 60

Dedication

This book is dedicated to

Bill and Lilly Reynolds
&
Matt Fahey
Who asked so little of life
and gave so much

Acknowledgments

For Liz DiVuolo and Mike DeRiggi
and their Fifth grade students
who listened so attentively to my words and
gave me the encouragement to keep on writing.
and
My Grandaughters
Sammantha
Who contributed the beautiful artwork
and hounded me until I completed our book
and
Nicole
Who contributed her beautiful words
and
Connor Cherney
(My Grandson)

All fall down

We go through life, we make mistakes
All fall down
We try to enter heaven's gates
All fall down
We are hateful to our fellow man
All fall down
We fail to lend a helping hand
All fall down
We cheat and lie to get ahead
All fall down
We'd rather cheat and lie instead
All fall down
We wonder why our children cry
We wonder why? Why?? Why??? Why????
We all fall down,
and down, down, below the ground yielding to life's refrain.

By: thom cherney, the janitor

Angels walk the hall

the angels of North Dover School
who walk the halls each day
scurrying along holding hands
as they go on their merry way
none have ever dreamed the dreams
or listened while they play
to that little voice inside their heads
that guides their steps each day
for what they see in their mind's eye
can be seen by only the chosen few
lost in the shadowy orb of day
transcending their flawed review
a choir invisible to guide and protect
always walking beside
and that chosen few always there
transcending their flawed review.

By: thom cherney, the janitor

As summer grows nigh

Early June, sun shining, flowers blooming, end of school year parties, picnics,
the bright green grass,
anticipation, excitement fill the air; giggles in the school hallways,
little feet run to and fro.
Talk of summer activities, vacations, water parks, camping trips or even a trip
to Disney
or visits to out - of state relitives.
The fifth grade student body prepairs to leave the farmilar to journey to the
less familiar
surroundings of their new schools in the fall,.
while the kindergarten class's journey to the cafetorium for the first time
in preparation for when they will start having lunch with the rest
of the school's students in september.
Baseball playing on the field behind the school, laughter from children playing
on the jungle gym.

As the North Dover family of teachers and staff welcome new faces
they prepair to bid a loving farewell to old friends.
Desks cleaned out, bookcases, globes and bulletin boards all covered with
bright colored paper in preparation for the summer respite,
all mark the end of the school year.

And then, "silence."

By: thom cherney, the janitor

As we travel

As we travel through this life
of mist and storm and shroud,
one can only ever hope
that mercy be endowed.
Life is but a single note,
a counterpoint in time.
So live each day in wonderment
of life's unending chime.

By: thom cherney, the janitor

At the back door

At the back school door children make their way
to start a new and bright school day.
The faces of children hiding their tears
with a feigned smile that masks their fears.
Parents rushed - to get along - driving away - singing their song.
Hypocrites come and hypocrites go
but little they know that a cold wind may blow
and change their lives forever,
and ever, and ever.
Amen.

By: thom cherney, the janitor

Bring in the clown

There is a man who comes each day
who walks the grounds and the school hallway
who always has a greeting smile
and takes the time to talk awhile
who tries to grant all the requests
at what he does he tries his best
but there is something down deep inside
that masks the hidden pain outside
for inside out and outside in
where does the duplicity begin?

for when it's said, said is done!
and once it's said, it can't be undone!
bring in the clown!

For roseanne

Love comes softly in times of sadness
like a warm breeze blowing across
the meandering river of thought or through
the shimmering leaves of the trees
along the banks of the mind

Love's soothing melody can resonate to the
depths of the human soul with the softness
of a feather or the tenderness of a loving touch.

By: thom cherney, the janitor

The Black Bird
By
Sammantha Dietrich

My Minds Eye

In my mind's eye i've seen it all
in my minds eye-i-see their fall
the daily routines that consume them all
going through life wanting it all
"send in the clowns"

They complicate their harried life
only adding to the horror of their daily strife
once a week they kneel and pray
that god will send good fortune their way
and if god don't deliver, the "others" will pay
well - it's certainly not my way
but then - who am-i-to say
let bells ring, let children sing
on the dark side of tomorrow
their hypocrisy goes deep
one man's lie is another man's truth
"send in the clowns"

By: thom cherney, the janitor

My brother never cried

Looking back on my childhood years
it seems i've cried a million tears
what i have seen through my eyes
despair - the pain - the human cries.

confusion reigned - there was no doubt
unable to grasp what life was about
peace eluded my troubled mind
what power worked god's human kind?
i lay in horror, with tear - filled eyes
but i never saw my brother cry.

the terror of life so close at hand
man's inhumanity to his fellow man
children cried their souls to keep
mothers cried themselves to sleep.

but i never saw my brother cry,
but then - he was always much stronger than i
my whole life now spent in tears
depression - confusion - all through the years
but i never saw my brother cry
but then again - he was always much tougher than i.

but in the late morning of a bright december day
i paid my brother a visit at his home along the bay
he spoke of a transition that he made along the way
we sat - and talked of years gone by - and the price we had to pay.

now time has passed and time has healed
most wounds that came our way
but no one - no one will ever, ever know the price we had to pay.

By: thom cherney, the janitor

My poems

My poems are written, as you will someday see
by someone else, surely not me

the thoughts that come to me each day

most are sad, seldom gay

there is a visitor by day or night
who brings me visions of pain and fright.

By: thom cherney, the janitor

My words

I write my words
with a transparent pen
that you can see right through
no hiding places for hate or greed
Period . . . .

By: thom cherney, the janitor

Parallel realities

One night—
as i lay in bed
in the downstairs room,
thought i
What's happening?
Am i really here?
i think-no-that's not it-i am here-but wait,
if i'm here, how can i be there?
God - what is it?
Is it the shadows? The others?
Oh! - i know
horror beyond all horrors!
Denigration of the psyche
i'm not really here - this is not real!
It can't be
go back, think!
That's not it either
but—but—what then?
Total confusion!
Contradiction heaped upon contradiction
hipocrasy beyond all hipocrasies.
Is what's happening to me really real?
Ah - what is real anyway?
The step across the string into hell is real,
really real - i know because i've been there, and back!
Maybe it will stop - this feeling of that is - this deep confounding intertwining
between the hell of my past, my reality in the here and now,
and my profound fear of the future,
not of death, but of life itself.
i must disconnect now,
slip back into "my" reality.

i can't think back anymore - or forward for that matter - it's slowly killing me!
Well anyway, let me go!
And, oh yeah, thank you God, for the childhood of misery - pain - and fear.
amen!

"As a traveler through this life, man but transcribes, transposes; he neither proscribes nor
proposes; he transmits the divinity of which we and the ages are but shadows."
Ralph Waldo Emerson

By: thom cherney, the janitor

perchance

baltimore, md

perchance i will remember you
and that dark and gloomy day

when the sunlight was taken
from my life
and you went far away

perchance i will remember your smile
to brighten up the gray

of that dark and gloomy afternoon
when you were taken away

By: thom cherney, the janitor

Please don't fight

(conversation with a little boy)

Please don't fight, not tonight, I have school tomorrow.
All life's dreams that fly me by, that I must catch and borrow.

I have no right to meager joys, by me be only sorrow.
When I dream tonight I will dream the dreams beyond the dreams of all life's pain
and sorrow.

As often is, as often was, the horror of life's victories.

I have no right to wish and hope, tomorrows deep - cut furrows.

In our soul it's said we can find peace, surcease of pain the morrow.
The will to live ebbs like the tide's release of pain and sorrow.

To each it is as to each it was, to travel the road before us.
I cannot yield to see life's joys and ponder peace the morrow.

For hope it's said to my account will gain full measure morose.

But all hope is gone, till I dream the dreams beyond the dreams of all
Life's pain and sorrow.

By: thom cherney, the janitor

10th Grade
By
Sammantha Dietrich

Rolling thunder

Let the drummers keep time
As the pipers play on
To the cycle's deep drone
As the caisson moves on
With flags at half staff
As the caisson moves on
Another Hero Has Gone
As the pipers play on
To the cycle's deep drone
As the caisson moves on

By: thom cherney, the janitor

second - hand pencils

second - hand pencils are sure to be found
like autumn leaves upon the ground
the classroom floors are littered each day
with the discards that are taken for granted.

it's with a well - chewed pencil and discarded scroll
is how my poems are written and stories told
it's at night when the classrooms are emptied out full
and the school is locked up for the day
that i wander the halls from class to class
seeking the bounty that's been thrown away.

care was not taken to tally their worth
their value not counted at all
second hand pencils have a story to tell
from the children who walk through the halls.

By: thom cherney, the janitor

The runner

I'm a runner day and night taking flight
ever since i can remember it's always been that way
trying to forget
forgetting to try
why?
i'll just take flight
again.
running from fear and fearing to run
no one knows but me
why is that so?
didn't they see?
didn't they know?

there were others just like me
didn't you see?
they were frightened just like me
they were running just like me
running, running just like me
he wanted others just like me
it was i who did not see.
his life is at its end now
you see?

should i stop this run?
it must end, you know
this run
it must be done.
so if it must end
i know
I'll do it tomorrow
or
tomorrow

or
tomorrow
but you see
tomorrow
never really comes.

well, in that case
if no one really cares
i'll wait
since no one really, really cares i'll wait
but don't worry
tomorrow
Will never come
because,
you know
it just won't.
tomorrow finally came
Now,
Peace?

By: thom cherney, the janitor

The man

the man who never was to be - no more than he became
whose life was always richly spent - on passionless goals and shame
he wasted all was given him on foolish folly's gain
the years went by
too late he found
he never had life's flame.

By: thom cherney, the janitor

The fall of man

Words - hurting words
lying in bed - at night - in the downstairs room
next to my brother
words - getting louder - dominating - resonating
hints of rage - hate - prejudice - bigotry
handed down
the horrid side of a mans cowardly nature
screams in the night
voices - loud voices
"DADDY I CRY"
sitting straight up in bed
fist like words - striking out, inflicting pain
"OH GOD I CRY"
"there is no god - there can't be-no-no
i didn't mean that-
GOD I'M SORRY"
(thinking that i too would be the recipient of a horrific beating)
hurting words - demeaning words
"AGAIN I CRY - DADDY"- "DADDY - ME - ASS" he screams!
lie down and go to sleep"- but we can't sleep
my brother strikes out in frustration - punching and kicking me with his bare
feet
Shut up he tells me!
i try to be quiet but there is such fright down deep in the very bowels of my
being
another voice screams out in pain and agony- please - please help me -
don't let him hurt me anymore
paralyzing words - demeaning words - no come back words
in the dead of night

where does it end?
it should have ended in the beginning!
words hurt - like fists
of this there is no doubt

"I would rather light a candle than curse the darkness"
Eleanor Roosevelt

By: thom cherney, the janitor

Mankind today

The
one single most threat to mankind today is
mankind today

By: thom cherney, the janitor

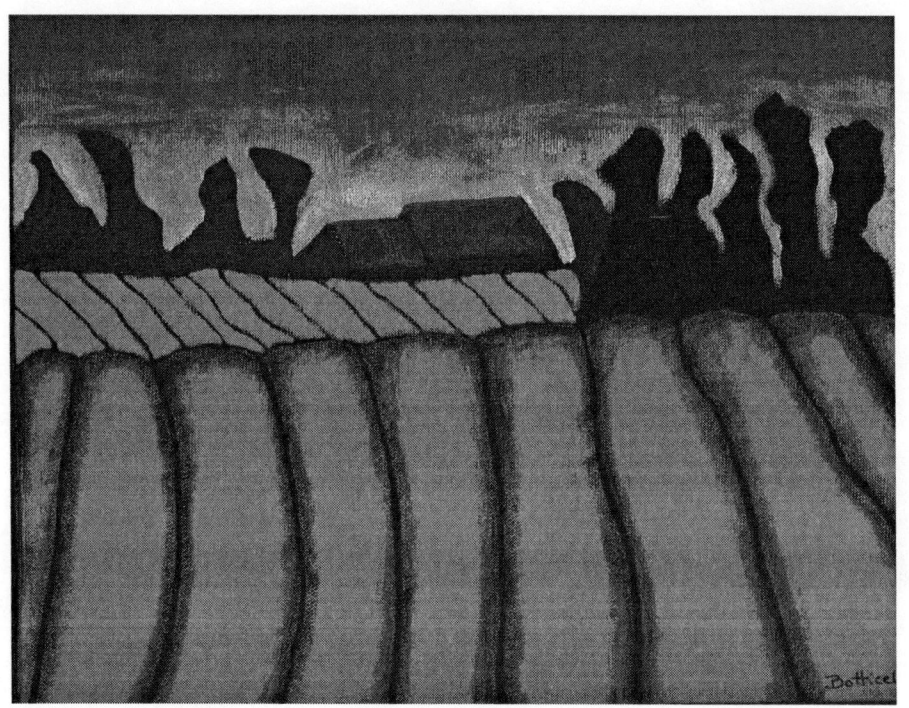

Uneasy Harvest
By
Donald Botticelli

the path of peace

(for robert)

broken pottery by the columbine path
of cobblestone and slate
just along the tall white fence
beyond the bright white garden gate
each time I pass the playground bench I stop to think awhile
of the little boy so full of life
and promise as a child
his beaming face, his helping hand
always willing to share
the old white elm
stands in silent grace
to welcome all who care
BE AT PEACE
sit down
for you are welcome here.

By: thom cherney, the janitor

The School Hallway

Walking down the school hallway
a little boy - sad - eyed - gaunt face
trying to force a smile
as we approach - hi Eric - how are you doing today?
fine he says - but I know he's not doing fine
as I look - his eyes reflect a deep unfeigned aching
we hesitate - just for a moment - just long enough to see
a little boy in turmoil - not quite knowing why he feels
the way he does - he stands - blank face - shoulders stooped
as if to ask
(as he watches all the other children - scurrying to class)
Why am I so sad?
what's wrong with me??
why can't I be happy???
(a little boy caught in the grip of something he can't understand)
not saying another word - he continues down the hallway to his classroom.

By: thom cherney, the janitor

HYPOCRITES

THE WORLD IS FULL OF HYPOCRITES
BUT DON'T THINK TOO POORLY OF THEM

THEY GO TO CHURCH TO SING AND PRAISE
AND PAY HOMAGE TO NO ONE

BUT AT LEAST THEY GO TO CHURCH
FOR WHAT IT'S WORTH

The worn "T" shirt

(Observation in the cafetorium)

The vocal class had their winter concert
last Thursday afternoon, the parents came
to claim the fame and sit in proud review.

The children stood on risers high,
all dressed to mark the day, their voices
echoed through the halls as the music played away.

Black and white were the colors they wore
all neat in fine array, except for one,
wearing a worn white "T" shirt, a little dingy and grey.

She stood behind some taller kids, her eyes welled up
with tears, hoping no one would notice, her embarrassment
and fears.

Her father was there in the audience, right in the very first
row, with that look of pride upon his face, a look only a
parent would know.

Then all at once he caught her eye and smiled at her as
though she was the only one on the stage, that look only a
child would know.

Then all at once her voice grew strong, her face was free
from fear, a father's love and encouragement echoed all
the love she'd known throughout the years.

She stood straight up with newfound strength,
her voice echoing through the halls, she stood and sang
with smiling face, as the music played along.

By: thom cherney, the janitor

trail of tears

there is no justice behind locked bars
that holds the prisoner there
they started life like all of us
but something happened
I know
despair
despair is something they know well
it was handed down
from generations long since gone
desperation bound
their long black trail of tears from
hell
in reach of heaven's gate
we go through life oblivious
obliged
to obliterate.

By: thom cherney, the janitor

what i have seen

(conversation with a parent)

what i have seen through my eyes
the hate, despair and human cries
the lack of love our children feel
who pray and yearn for something real
confusion rules our lot today
but who's to blame?
who's to pay?

we pray our children grow up well
we speak of heaven - death and hell
when children ask why is this so?
the loving parent does not know
confusion rules our lot today
but who's to blame?
who's to pay?

i've seen the hate in every guise
i've seen despair and heard the cries
i give the love a child must feel
i try to give them something real
the child strikes out - in deep despair
searching for someone to care

our youth is searching for a way
but who's to blame?
who's to pay?

By: thom cherney, the janitor

Why?

Why are we waiting?
Our world can't stand the strain
Our children wince with pain

Environment
The ocean groans
The forest moans
The earth cannot transcend
Man's futile selfish ends

But still we will not bend
We're racing head - on toward the end
We're using up their time
We need to look behind
Our forward thrusts unwind
Our selfish deeds combine
But still we seldom look behind

Our ecosystems fail
Global warming hails
We can see it from afar
We believe we're better than we are

But in reality we're the problem
Not the solution
We're the cause of all pollution

Just look! Look! - You won't look
Because you know! - You know!
You know you have no feel - no love
No connection — you show no remorse
Feel no pain - YOU LOOK UP!!

Look around
You who are supposed to be
Our guardian - our protector
The stewards of our earth
Listen! Listen! to our earth

So don't be sad, our future
You will make it right
The elder's day will come
So we must wait - wait
It's not too late
So you, our future
Speak to our earth and listen - listen
and wait
your time will come

BUT REMEMBER
WHAT DAMAGE HAS BEEN DONE TO THIS EARTH
IN THE PAST WILL BE RETURNED
IN KIND IN THE FUTURE!!!

By: thom cherney, the janitor

Alberto
By
Sammantha Dietrich

"whys and therefores"

the whys and therefores
are there to be
a guide for all humanity

but the whys and therefores
tend to change
with acts of greed
and hate deranged

as time goes by with great disdain
the mounting hours record their pain

the elders' hour has not yet come
to change their plight
and run the run

By: thom cherney, the janitor

Reality

This person you see in your world is not me.
I have a difficult time dealing with your reality.
Each time I try to be the real me,
my world collides with yours,
don't you see?
So I reinvent me, constantly.
It's how I survive in your world,
don't you see?
Perception is "reality."

By: thom cherney, the janitor

I awoke

I woke this night in deep despair
from a sleep so troubled and grim
and as I woke the sound of angels
and a choir of cherubim
was
there to protect
my anguished soul so far away and safe
there was no reason for me to run
no reason
no need to take flight
i love the stillness of the night
and all the wisdom it brings
that life has taken from my thoughts
like a thief sneaking by in the night
i'll go back now with the others
so close yet so far away
i'll go back with the crows that caw in the tree
that lull me to sleep each night.

By: thom cherney, the janitor

I'll walk to the river

I'll walk to the river today,
through this caravan park,
past the trailer homes.
Tan one blue
Green one brown
Light brown one with the dark brown shutters
that don't shut.
Past the turquoise one with doors that don't lock,
because the occupant can't find the key.
Past the white one with the blue shutters
where Mr. John McVey lived before he died.
Past the faded green one with the peeling paint
and the car in the driveway that don't run anymore.
Past the blue one with the weeds growing up
through the stones in the yard.
Past the green one with the flagpole in the front yard
and the tattered flag at perpetual half mast
in honor of a grandson who will not be coming home from Iraq.
Past the dark tan one where the old lady feeds the neighborhood cats
(and the occasional opossum).
Past the faded pink one with the old rusted wheelchair under the overhang
next to the front steps.

Yes, I will walk to the river today
like many days past and many days to come.
Past the trailer homes with the for - sale signs in their windows
where death looms heavy.

Past the clubhouse
where the residents gather daily
to pick up their mail
share idle conversation
and look at the bulletin board
with notices of things for sale:

Car '92 Chev. Low miles "best offer"
Walker, almost new, cheap
Wheelchair, but a year old, make offer.

Yes, I will walk to the river again today
past the caravans old and new.
Past the clubhouse
where the lonely and soon to - be - lonely gather.

Another day
like many other days past and yet to come.

Yes, I'll walk to the river again today
and sit on the bench, all alone,
watching the crystal brown river water rush by,
waiting, waiting, for another day
to come, and go.
Yes,. I will walk to the river again,
today.

By: thom cherney, the janitor

The Doorkeeper

(Introspection)

i remember lonely days
old peeling lead paint on the ceiling
drab colorless walls with cobwebs growing in the corners
exposed water and steam pipes running helter skelter
throughout the cold lonely cellar apartment
the pungent odor of cigarette smoke
the lingering smell of alcohol
the odor of kerosene hanging heavy in the air
sleepless nights in my cellar room
what was I to do?
and when at long last sleep did come, so came the nightmares,
voices, loud voices giving way to whispers, shadows in my mind
and upon waking in the morning the odor and wetness beneath
me and the presence, the body odor surrounding and overwhelming
me, the stark terror - filled realization that i was a prisoner
captured like an animal with nowhere to run,
and the loneliness, oh the loneliness
at times I cried myself to sleep
praying that someone, anyone would help me
but it was not to be, my fate was sealed
but then one day i found an escape deep within myself.
i just left and went to the other place, a serene and quiet place
where birds sang and chirped and a warm fragrance filled the air
where everything was peaceful.

thom cherney, the janitor

The Doorkeeper

April 1st 2009

(off kilter)

The day was filled with excitement
The world was all aglow
There was magic in the air
But, but why are you crying, little boy?
                        (Asked the kindly old man)
I don't know, answered the boy.

Did someone hurt you? asked the man.
        No, answered the boy. No, Asked the man,
                        But why are you crying?
I don't know, answered the little boy with tears welling up
in his eyes.

There must be some reason for crying, said the man.
        The little boy answered,
                The world makes me very sad
                        and
                I cry, answered the little boy.

Alter ego - another aspect of one's personality,
        an intimate friend or constant companion.

                        thom cherney, the janitor

Peace
By
Sammantha Dietrich

Mortality

I wax friendly faces of past lives,
to memory commit a life such as mine,
i succumb to the tribute paid the gods
their rightful due,
to expend life at will,
with no sense of shame,
no remorse to abide by
on earth or in the heavens

where I come from I shall soon return
without hesitation,
this life is but a cinder in the eye of fate,
which takes us back to times forgotten in our lives
and past lives.

to understand life's meaning which at times has no meaning
to those who have not the essence of life ingrained
in their minds, their hearts or to the very depths of their bowels.
to live a purposeful life,
this essence must be ingrained, it must be there,
their very being demands this.

as travelers through this life
we are but mere shadows in a universe of shadows.

I come to grips with life today
who's to say how it began
or how it will end,
only the gods above or below know this for certain.

By: thom cherney, the janitor

To bow at the altar of conformity

Don't do it,
It's not worth it! Cried the poet.
Be your own person,
Be vigilant, be informed,
Reason things out,
Don't believe the demigods,

If you stand up for what's morally right in life:
First
they will ignore you
then
they will laugh at you
then
they will fight you
then
They will ask you to compromise
Don't do it
and then
you will win!

?

Untitled

I remember Olympics on the couch,
but I forget winning an event.
I remember reading your letters aloud,
but I forget the ones I sent.
I remember our camp outs on the floor,
but I forget the games we'd play
I remember the fun times we'd have,
but I forget to call you every day.
I remember the fights late each night,
but I forget how they'd begin.
I remember playing bronco bull,
but I forget who would win.
I remember the times you left us home,
but I forget just how long.
I remember listening to Nirvana all day,
but I forget the song.
I remember leaving hotels so late,
but I forget just why,
I remember you saying you'd be okay,
but I forget why I would cry.
I remember the smell of the hospital,
but I forget the time of night.
I remember you'll always be over my shoulder,
but I forget, was it left or right.

By: Nicole Dietrich

Untitled

Dirty carpets and windows
covered by sheets
TV blaring
an eerie glow
upon a couch
blanketed by a young girl
eyes wide open
glaring
rain hitting the glass in the dark of the night.

A rapping on the door
paint peeling
water dripping
the sound of silence so inviting
the door creaking
feet scrambling
a voice booms through the air
she pulls herself to her feet
running
the terror sprayed across her face
a deer trapped in gleaming headlights.

She locks herself away from sight
heart pounding
fingers trembling
shivers through her body
she alone can hear the whimpers
voices cutting through the air
holding back tears

keeping still in the dark.
Light shines through
windows
covered by sheets
out from the still
her door creaks open
and she crawls into the light.

By: Nicole Dietrich

The Dreamer
By
Sammantha Dietrich

Untitled

I am from sunsets in freehold
and manhunt in the dark
the bottle - cap club
and pool - hopping in the summer.

I am from broken summers
and parties went to waste
my motor home leaving
and six months without my dad.

I am from hot concrete
and the ice cream jingle
the sixteenth block
and bagel day.

I am from first floor apartments
with Maria and Irene
empty pools
and singing in art.

I am from switching schools
and making friends
nine different houses
and sitting home alone.

I am from sharing bunk beds
and trashed kitchens
broken dressers
and fights at 2 am.

I am from hot summer days
and cool ocean blues
breakfast at Freedman's
and nights around the pool.

I am from biking on boardwalks
and fireworks on the beach
cool sands underneath me
and holding hands in the back seat.

I am from late night parties
and "cute" pictures
skinny - dipping in hot tubs
and sleepless nights.

I am from fourteen months of holding back
and countless arguments
buying extra presents around the holidays
and exchanging "I love you's."

I am from crying and giggling
and hugging New Year's Eve
from burlapping all night
and forgetting my worries.

I am from secrets and scandal
half - truths and lies
rumors around me
and friends left behind.

I'm from fights with teachers
a hundred in algebra
to sitting on stage in June
and leaving Belmar behind.

By: Nicole Dietrich

Get Published, Inc!
Thorofare, NJ 08086
23 September 2009
BA2009266